“Jesus is Victor!”

Blumhardt’s Battle with the Powers of Darkness
A historical account
By Pastor Johann Christoph Blumhardt

JOHANN CHRISTOPH BLUMHARDT

(1805 - 1880)

Village Archives, Bad Boll, Germany.

GOTTLIEBIN DITTUS
(1815 - 1872)

Bruderhof Historical Archives, Walden, NY, USA.

JESUS IS VICTOR!

BLUMHARDT'S BATTLE
WITH THE POWERS OF DARKNESS

JOHANN CHRISTOPH BLUMHARDT

FORWORDS BY KEVIN DEDMON & WALTER HEIDENREICH

Translation from the original German manuscript
Edited by Stephan Krueger
Layout and Cover design by Guiding Productions

Published by AwakenMedia.de
Postfach 1132
Ebersbach an der Fils, Germany

ISBN: 978-3-945339-11-4

1st Edition

www.awakenmedia.de

FOREWORD BY KEVIN DEDMON

Johann Christoph Blumhardt was one of the first catalysts of the modern-day healing movement. I believe it is vital that we know the history of breakthrough that others fought for, so that we can understand the keys to tearing down strongholds for our generation. Moreover, when we read about those who pioneered Kingdom principles in practical ways, we are not just reading for information, but for impartation as well. When we honor the prophet or the righteous man, we receive their reward. In other words, when we value someone else's victory by reading about it, we get a reward/impartation to go to the next levels of breakthrough for our lives.

I believe that as you read this book of Blumhardt's breakthrough, you will be positioned to receive more healing breakthrough for yourself and others. I want to encourage you to buy this book, read it, and then do it!

I believe God is looking for the next Johann Christoph Blumhardt who will go to the next levels of Kingdom breakthrough. That could be you!

Kevin Dedmon, Author, *The Ultimate Treasure, Unlokking Heaven, The Risk Factor* & *Firestarters*

FOREWORD BY WALTER HEIDENREICH

"But if it is by the Spirit of God that I drive out demons, then the kingdom of God has come upon you." (Matt. 12:28)

"You know...how God anointed Jesus of Nazareth with the Holy Spirit and power, and how he went around doing good and healing all who were under the power of the devil, because God was with him. We are witnesses of everything he did." (Acts 10:37-39)

When Jesus set me free from my drug addiction, it was the first time that I had experienced the all-pervading, liberating power of God in my life for real. From then on I only wanted one thing – to live in this power and to share it with others. And that's what I've been doing, now for more than forty years. I was and still am utterly fascinated by how Jesus moved in the power of God as he healed and delivered people. On my quest to discover more about the men and women who helped shape revival history, I also came across the book by Johann Christoph Blumhardt. I was deeply moved by this simple pastor from Möttlingen's unwavering perseverance in his mission to free the woman Gottliebin from the enemy's clutches. This story, with its resulting, sustained period of revival, had a lasting influence on me.

The book you are now reading is a fascinating and thrilling look at the life of Johann Christoph Blumhardt and is an encouragement not only to trust in the unchanging power of the love of God, but also in the power to be found in serving people and nations today. The power of the Kingdom of God and the signs and wonders which followed in the life of Johann Christoph Blumhardt encourage us to both preach and demonstrate the Kingdom as well as to seek this power today. An important book, particularly in view of today's often so power-less Christianity. May it help many, as they seek this God of love, to discover and experience Him as He really is.

Thank you, Stephan!

Walter Heidenreich, *President of FCJG International*

INTRODUCTION BY GARY S. GREIG

During the latter half of the 19th century, what God did through Johann Christoph Blumhardt represents a major epicenter of a move of the Holy Spirit to restore Jesus' healing ministry to the Body of Christ that spanned Russia, Europe, and North America.

Blumhardt and other latter 19th-century Faith Healing leaders (Rein, Trüdel, Stockmayer, Baxter, et al.) directly impacted, and imparted healing models and Holy Spirit anointing to, leaders of the North American Faith Cure Movement (Cullis, Boardman, Simpson, et al.), and this served as a precursor to the Pentecostal outpouring of the Holy Spirit at the turn of the 20th century. Also during the latter half of the 19th century, the Holy Spirit moved in healing power through the Eastern Orthodox healing priest, Father John Sergieff (also known as St. John of Kronstadt) that greatly impacted thousands for Christ and His kingdom in 19th-century pre-Bolshevik Russia. The Holy Spirit moved in power through Fr. John Sergieff of Kronstadt at the same time that He moved through Blumhardt in Germany, and in the Faith Cure Movement leaders in North America, Switzerland, and Britain.

God was preparing the Body of Christ globally to advance His Kingdom through healing signs and wonders that confirm that Jesus is Healer and Supreme Victor over Satan (Matt. 12:25-28; Mark 16:20; Acts 10:38; Col. 2:13-15) in the face of the satanic onslaughts that came in the 20th century in the Bolshevik Revolution, atheistic communism, occultic Nazism, and the two World Wars that collectively took millions of lives. Healing signs and wonders have always been God's method of confirming His Word by His power (Jer. 32:20; Matt. 10:7-8; 28:19-20; 1 Cor. 2:4-5; 4:20). It is significant that the Holy Spirit not only began to restore healing ministry to the experience of the European and North American Church through Johann Christoph Blumhardt's ministry, but He also used Blumhardt to influence the Biblical Theology Movement leaders (Barth, Niebuhr, Moltmann, et al.) to counter German liberal, Christ-denying theology with a return to affirming the Word of God, written in Scripture, and manifested in the historical Jesus Christ. Wherever the Holy Spirit works in power from the Early Church to the present day, people's hearts are powerfully turned to God and His Word, lives are healed and purified, and Jesus is glorified as Lord of all.

My wife Catherine and I have seen Jesus heal almost every person on the streets that we have prayed over for the past two years. He connected us to Todd White (Lifestyle Christianity) and other street healing leaders (Pete Cabrera Jr., Tom Loud, Doug Collins), whose many YouTube videos inspired us. We have been amazed how easy it is to see Jesus heal people on the streets outside of the church if we just lose our fear of man and pray over people. So many were healed in libraries, coffee shops, auto shops, gas stations, etc., as we prayed for their pains and sicknesses, saw the Holy Spirit cause healing to manifest right there in their bodies, and then shared Jesus' love with them. Jesus showed us afresh that He can use any believer to heal pain and sickness: this is the normal Christian life, not a special gift (Matt. 10:7-8 "**proclaim** ... and **heal**"; 28:19-20 "make disciples … teaching them to **obey** everything I have **commanded you**")[1]. We've seen more people healed on the streets in past two years than we ever saw healed in the past 29 years in church and in three seminaries (Fuller, Regent, United Theological Seminary) in which I used to teach men and women preparing for the ministry (we've been in healing prayer ministry in our church and in seminaries for 29 years). Jesus is amazing!

Gary S. Greig, Ph.D. *The University of Chicago, 1990, Near Eastern Languages and Civilizations; Director, Three Oaks of Mamre Educational and Charitable Trust; former faculty member, Fuller Theological Seminary, Regent University School of Divinity, United Theological Seminary.*

---

[1] Emphasis added by the author.

PREFACE BY JOHANN CHRISTOPH BLUMHARDT

(TO THE ROYAL CONSISTORY)

As I hand the accompanying report to a highly praiseworthy synod, I feel pressed to declare that I have not yet spoken as boldly and forthrightly to anyone about my experiences. My best friends have their doubts about me and brought me into the embarrassing situation of having to be completely silent toward them. It is as though they feared the danger of even hearing about this case, although I am grateful to them that they trembled for me continually during my battle. Since up to now most of it has remained a secret, I could keep it in my chest until my grave without telling about it. Therefore, I was completely free to pick and choose for this report, and it would have been easy for me to give such a report, as anyone could have read without stumbling in any way. But I could not do this, and although I trembled through every paragraph, thinking whether it might not be hasty and careless to tell everything so clearly, I felt the urge within me again and again, "Tell it all."

Therefore, I dare to do it, and do it in the Name of Jesus, who is Victor. I consider it not only my duty to be honest and open toward my highly honored synod, which has deserved every right of openness on my part, but also toward my Lord Jesus, whose cause alone it was for which I had to do battle. Of course, you will understand my wish that this report be kept more as a private communication, since I speak here for the first time without reservation, in the same way as a trusted friend confides his secrets in the bosom of his friends. I do not even have an easily readable copy of this report, and I doubt that I will feel led soon to read it to anyone. For this reason, I trust the more that you will respect my request to prevent publicity for the time being. Only twice did I tell anything circumstantial, and then only peripheral matters. Once in Calw and the other time in Vaihingen, before colleagues who seemed to be disposed toward me in a friendly way; and at least in the latter place, I burned my fingers. But this report proves that I am not afraid otherwise to come out into the light.

A second request is to be pardoned: may the readers read the whole more than once before they pronounce judgment. In the meantime, I trust in Him, who holds all souls in His power. No matter what the judgments might be, I have the satisfaction of having spoken the truth without guile and on top of that the rock-solid certainty, "Jesus is Victor."

1

The above-mentioned Gottliebin Dittus is single, without means, and twenty-eight years old. She has lived together with two sisters and one brother, who is half blind. All are older than she. They have lived together for four years in a modest first-floor apartment in Möttlingen. Due to her good disposition and her faithful education by Christian parents, she has a good basic education, even though her school training was not the best. The instruction she received through my predecessor, Pastor Dr. Barth, now living in Calw, brought a good Christian foundation into her heart. She remembers him with gratitude at every opportunity. After finishing school, she had a desire for the world at first, but her reputation was always unsullied. She worked as a servant in several places and is remembered to this day with high esteem in the houses she served, because of her proved faithfulness, especially in Weil der Stadt, where she was for eight years.

Due to a peculiar disease of the kidneys which she suffered from during the years 1836-1838, her Christian disposition became more decided and more serious. During this illness many and highly respected doctors attempted to treat her at the recommendation of Pastor Dr. Barth and Vicar Stotz. This happened just before I was installed here; that is, in July of 1838. Since then she has remained here in Möttlingen and has led a retiring and quiet life with her brother and sisters. She was loved and respected for her Christian understanding. Gottliebin retained a number of physical weaknesses from her disease, one being that she could never pass water without a special instrument given her by her doctor. The disease also left her with a shorter foot, a high side, stomach trouble, etc.

As soon as she first entered into the above-mentioned apartment, into which she moved in February of 1840, Gottliebin believed, as she told me later, to have felt a peculiar influence on her. This struck her the more since she thought she saw and heard many weird and sinister things. Even her brother and sisters took note of this. Right from the first day, when she prayed at the table, "Come, Lord Jesus, be our guest…" she had fits in which she fell to the floor, unconscious. What was heard was a frequently recurring trampling and scuffling in the bedroom, the living room, and the kitchen. At times these noises lasted all night and often scared the poor brother and sisters very much. They also disquieted the people living upstairs, even though all of them shied away from letting anything about these things become known. Gottliebin experienced special things in her body. For example, at night her hands were folded by force; she saw figures and small lights, etc. It appears from her accounts that the later possessions had their beginning in her even at this time. From this time on she had something repulsive and inexplicable in her behaviour and a repugnant way about her, which was disliked in many places. But everyone let it go, because no one asked much about this poor orphan family. Also, Gottliebin was highly reticent about her strange experiences. It was not until the fall of 1841 that Gottliebin came to me at the parsonage because her nightly temptations had reached an ever higher degree. However, she spoke only in general terms about her temptations so that I could not get anything worthwhile out of her. Nor could I give her very satisfactory advice. On the other hand, she confessed freely something about her former life because she hoped to get free from the aforementioned temptations through this confession. In December of that year and until February of 1842, she suffered from erysipelas in her face and lay dangerously ill. Through the entire time of her illness I did not care much to visit her because her behavior repulsed me. She would look at me out of the corner of her eyes, would not respond to my greetings or unfold her hands, which she had folded before, when I prayed; and would not pay any attention to my words. She would even seem nearly unconscious, which she was not before or after my visits. I thought of her then as a self-willed, self-righteous and spiritually proud person, even as others began to think of her. Therefore, I stayed away rather than to expose myself to a lot of embarrassments. Meanwhile, she received faithful medical treatment, and at the end she recuperated.

Finally, in April of 1842, I learned for the first time something about the ghost in the house. Two of Gottliebin's relatives had come to ask my advice because it could not be kept secret any longer, as the whole neighborhood had noticed the trampling at night. At that time, Gottliebin saw with special frequency the figure of a woman of this town (who had died two years earlier), holding a dead child in her arms. Gottliebin carefully kept her name secret and did not tell it to me until later. This woman, she said, would always stand at the same place in front of her bed and at times would move toward her and then would often repeat these words, "I want to be left alone," or, "Give me a paper, and I won't come back," etc. Now I was asked whether anything more specific could be inquired of this woman figure. My advice was that Gottliebin was not to start a conversation with the figure under any circumstances, all the more since no one could know how much self-deception was part of it. One thing was sure — anyone who became involved with the spirit world could get into terrible error and foolishness. Also, Gottliebin was to pray seriously and faithfully, and the whole thing would stop by itself after a while. Upon my request a friend of hers dared to sleep in her house. (One of Gottliebin's sisters was serving in a household outside the city at that time, and her brother was only rarely at home and her other sister was not enough.) She also heard the trampling and finally, guided by the shimmer of a light, they discovered half a piece of paper under a bed, at the threshold of the bedroom door. It was covered with soot and all written upon. But the writing could not be read because of the soot smeared on it. Next to it, they found three crown thalers and a number of smaller coins, each one wrapped in paper by itself and smeared with soot. That writing seemed to be a prescription, possibly of magic. From that point on there was quiet in the house for about a fortnight. However, the trampling started again. A light flickering on the floor behind the stove revealed a whole number of things which had been buried there. (Immediately underneath the living room floor was the ground.) There was found a box of little flasks, chalk, salt, bones, etc. Furthermore, small square pieces of paper containing little powders were found together with other pieces of paper in which were wrapped three or four small coins each, all disfigured by soot in a most ugly way. The things which could be analyzed, like the powders, were later analyzed chemically by the chief medical examiner and an apothecary in Calw. However, neither one discovered anything special, and therefore, I burned the whole discovery except for the money. I thought the strange affair would thus be ended, which, however, was not at all the case.

In the meantime, the trampling assumed such proportions that everyone was excited by it. One could hear it during the day as well as at night, often when no one was in the living room. Passersby were scared, especially when Gottliebin was inside, because the noise occurred in front of her and behind her, even on the table, shaking it violently. Often this happened in the presence of others. The physician, Dr. Späth of Merklingen, who had always treated her with compassion and to whom alone she had confided many things, stayed in the living room for a night on two occasions, together with other curious persons. What he experienced was more than what he had expected. The whole thing not only became the talk of the town, but spread about in the whole region so that tourists began arriving out of curiosity. Finally, fearing such a great tumult, I decided to make nightly investigations in the house. I made a secret agreement with the mayor of the town, carpet-manufacturer Kraushaar, a sensible, sober, and God-fearing man; and several men of the town council, altogether some six to eight men. We divided ourselves into parties of two in and around the house and arrived, unexpected, around ten o'clock in the evening. Mose Stanger, a young, married man, also a relative of Gottliebin's, a man distinguished by Christian discernment and having the best of reputation in other respects, later my most faithful helper, had gone there before us. As soon as I entered the living room, two very loud bangs met me from the bedroom. In a short time, others followed. Noises, bangs, and knockings of the most varied kind were heard, mostly in the bedroom, where Gottliebin lay on her bed, fully dressed. The other guards outside and upstairs heard everything and met downstairs after some time, because they had become convinced that everything they heard originated there. The tumult seemed to increase, especially after I had asked that a hymn be sung and had prayed a short prayer. In the space of three hours, twenty-five bangs were heard from a certain spot in the bedroom. They were so loud that the chair leaped, the windows rattled, and sand fell from the ceiling. Villagers at a far distance were reminded of the shooting on New Year's Eve. Beside these bangs, softer and louder noises were heard, some like the tapping of fingers, or a more or less regular drumming. One could follow the sound, which seemed to begin mainly under the dresser, and reach after it with one's hand without noticing the least thing. We tried it with and without light, but it did not change anything. However, the loudest bangs occurred only when all of us were in the living room. One could clearly make out the place under the door from which the bangs came. Everything was checked in greatest detail, but no explanation could be found by any method. Finally, toward one o'clock in the morning, when all of us were in the living room, Gottliebin called me to her bedside and asked if she could say who the figure was if it appeared, as she could already hear some scuffling. I denied her that entirely. I had already had my fill of the investigation, and I did not want to risk the possibility that this many people were going to see something inexplicable. Therefore, I asked her to get up. I finished the investigation and made provision that Gottliebin could immediately find room and board in another house. Thus we left the house. The half-blind brother was supposed to have heard and seen many things after we left. Strange to say, the noise was loudest during the night we visited there.

2

The following day was a Friday, and Gottliebin was present at the service of that day. Half an hour later an incredible crowd had gathered in front of her house, and a messenger told me that she was in a deep faint and near death. I rushed there and found her lying on her bed, quite stiff. The skin of her head and arms was glowing and trembling, but the rest of her appearance indicated suffocation. The living room was crowded and, a doctor who happened to be there from another village had rushed in, trying this and that to bring her back to life. But soon he left, shaking his head. After about half an hour she awakened and told me quietly that she had seen the figure of the woman with the dead child in the living room when she returned from church. But soon after, she had fainted. In the afternoon of that day we dug on the spot where the blows had fallen. The bottom boards lay on the floor without being fastened. It was done by men of confidence and in my presence. When Mose Stanger touched the place which was of chief interest with his hand, a flame shot up there and Mose backed away. Upon further investigation we first found a number of small pieces of paper like those mentioned above, together with powders and small packages of money, and finally a pot which had the bottom of another pot for a cover and which contained small bones mixed with earth. The appearance of the figure with the dead child had already caused to spread the legend that it was the murderer of a child whose dead body could be found in the ground. The grave digger who was with us insisted that he recognized the bones, on which there was still some flesh, as the bones of a child. In order to prevent all embarrassment, I packed all of these things together and went, accompanied by the mayor, to the chief medical examiner, Herr Dr. Kaiser, at Calw. We told him everything openly. He stated that the bones were those of a bird. Therefore, all of the things we had found thus far pointed to the fact that sometime ago some black magic must at least have been attempted, and that now the dead were disquieted because of it. As I learned then, birds and especially ravens are frequently used by the common people in a superstitious way for the purpose of secret magic.

Now my chief desire was to suppress forever all things that would cause a tumult. I provided room and board for Gottliebin at another place in the house of one of her cousins, and later in the house of another cousin, the father of Mose, a member of the town council, who was also her godfather. He had a large family. At that time, four grown daughters and two sons lived in his house. The whole family was of Christian disposition, very compassionate with Gottliebin, and guarded the utmost silence. Furthermore, I asked Gottliebin not to go back to her house, if possible, for the time being. She did not move back into it until the middle of the following year. No more fuss could be made about this affair, and I told myself that I would make completely secret visits to her home from time to time, together with the mayor and some other sensible men in order to see what would come of it. I had a special horror of the appearances of somnambulism, which so frequently caused unpleasant attention and up to now had produced so little good. And since a mysterious and dangerous field opened up before me, I could not but commend the thing to the Lord in my solitary prayers. I asked Him to preserve me and others from all foolishness and errors into which one might be tempted to get involved. When the matter developed into something more serious, I had special prayer and counsel in my room with the mayor and Mose, and I can say that a sober disposition was kept among us because of this, which alone could promise a blessed ending for us. A number of weeks passed before the uproar in the region ceased. Many tourists came to visit the house. Many wanted to sleep in it at night in order to convince themselves of the truth of the things that had been reported. However, the house was carefully kept under surveillance, which was easier to do since the village policeman lived right across from it. On one occasion three Roman Catholic priests from the neighborhood of Baden wanted to spend a number of hours in the living room at night. When I was asked, I rejected such requests decisively. Slowly things quieted down and the entire following part has remained outside of the knowledge of the community, even though people noticed here and there that things were still not right, but only infrequently, because the people were afraid. Once in a while they spied on the house and had pity on me, but on the whole they do not know anything certain and coherent up to this day. The trampling in the house did not stop completely until the beginning of this year (1844) and was especially violent on the days of prayer and repentance of our church. Also, various figures were constantly noted; likewise small lights creeping along the wall. I cannot guarantee these reports since I myself have never seen anything of that sort.

3

The above-mentioned investigation took place on the third of June of 1842. Soon I heard that the trampling continued, even in the other house Gottliebin lived in, and that as soon as something was heard, she usually would fall into violent convulsions. These became ever stronger and longer-lasting, so that many times she would hardly be free for five minutes in between. I visited her as her spiritual counselor. She declared at that occasion that something was floating in front of her eyes that made her rigid. When I prayed with her, she fainted and sank back on her bed. Once I saw her in convulsions when the doctor was present. Her whole body trembled and every muscle in her head and her arms was in violent motion, although she was rigid and stiff otherwise. Often foam would flow out of her mouth. She was lying like this for several hours, and the doctor who had never seen anything like this seemed to be helpless. But suddenly she awakened, sat up and drank water and one could hardly believe she was the same person. In this fashion things went on for several days. On a Sunday night I went there again when a number of her women friends were present and silently watched her terrible convulsions. I sat down at some distance. She twisted her arms, turned her head to the side and bent her body up high. Foam flowed again from her mouth. It had become clear to me that something demonic played a role here after what had happened so far, and it hurt me to think that there should be no means or help in such a horrible affair. While I was in these thoughts, a sort of wrath gripped me. I jumped forward, took her stiff hands, pulled her fingers together with force as for prayer, loudly spoke her name into her ear in her unconscious state and said, "Fold your hands and pray, 'Lord Jesus, help me!' We have seen long enough what the devil is doing; now we also want to see what Jesus can do!"

After a few moments she awakened, prayed those words after me, and all convulsions ceased, to the great surprise of those present. This was the decisive moment which pulled me into activity for the cause with irresistible power. Before I had not had the slightest thought of it. Now a pressing impulse led me, which still is so fresh in my mind that later on it was often my only consolation, because it convinced me that I had not acted out of my own choice or presumption in a matter whose horrid development I could never have realized in my mind then.

When she had come to, I comforted her and prayed some more with her and left orders when I departed that I was to be called in case the convulsions returned. At ten o'clock that night a messenger came to me in a great hurry and said she had had a quiet evening until just now when the convulsions had seized her more violently than ever. When I got to her, the nurse seemed to be at the point of fainting, because the spectacle was ghastly above measure. Immediately I tried the above procedure, and the effect was the same within moments. I was just about to leave when she suddenly fell backwards on her bed. Immediately I made her call out the same words, "Lord Jesus, help me!" Although she could hardly get them out, she came to again, and the convulsions did not break out again. But at that moment the whole thing started all over, and thus it continued for three hours until she called out, "Now I am quite well." She had a quiet night then and the whole next day until the fits started again at nine o'clock that night. This time I remained with her for several hours, as I did nearly always later on, together with the mayor and Mose Stanger. It could already be noticed that something hostile in her was directing itself against me. Her eyes opened widely. She made a horrible face which did not express anything but wrath and rage. She clenched her fists and made threatening motions at me. Then she held her open hands close to my eyes as if she wanted to rip out both of my eyes quickly, etc. In all of that I remained firm and immobile, prayed short prayers, mostly after Bible verses, and did not pay any attention to threats. These were so ineffectual that never, not even when she rushed towards me with a great threat, did she ever even touch me. Finally, the whole thing passed when with great force she thrashed repeatedly with both her arms on the bed. It looked as though a spiritual power exuded from her fingertips. Afterwards she reportedly saw all sorts of figures in front of her which did not leave until after a while. This continued repeatedly with interruptions of one to three days, and at the end this kind of convulsion ceased entirely.

I was already beginning to have hope, when I was told that one could hear that same tapping as with fingers around Gottliebin. Then suddenly she would receive a blow on the chest and would sink back, and then she would see the same female figure which she had seen in her own apartment. According to her statements, the figure was that of a widow who had died two years before and who had no relatives. She had only left two sisters who were dead by then. When she was on her deathbed her conscience bothered her a great deal and she confessed serious sins to me, but found little peace before she died. When I went to Gottliebin's house with my usual companions (because I never wanted to go there without reliable eye and ear witnesses) I soon really heard those spooky noises. She herself was lying on her bed,

was conscious and felt no trouble. Suddenly it seemed as if something went into her, and her whole body began to move. I then prayed some and mentioned the name of Jesus. Immediately she rolled her eyes, banged her hands together and said with a voice which could instantly be recognized as not being hers, not only because of the tone but because of the expression and character of it, "I cannot stand to hear that Name." All were horrified. I had never heard anything like it and silently turned to God that He might grant me wisdom and caution and guard me especially from untimely curiosity. Finally, I dared to ask some questions with the firm resolution to limit myself to the most necessary and to watch my emotions in case my curiosity might get the better of me. In reference to that woman, I asked her questions something like this:
"Don't you rest in the grave?" "No."
"Why not?"
"That is the reward for my deeds."
"Didn't you," I continued, silently supposing that it was that person, "confess all of your sins to me?"
"No, I murdered two children and buried them in the field."
"Don't you know of any help now? Can't you pray?"
"I cannot pray."
"Don't you know Jesus Who forgives sins?"
"I can't stand to hear that Name."
"Are you alone?"
"No."
"Who is with you?"

The voice answered with hesitation, then with a rush, "The worst of all."

The conversation continued thus for a while, and the talking person accused herself of magic, for whose sake she was bound to the devil. Already seven times, she said, she had come out, but now she would not come out any more. I asked her whether I might pray for her. She did not allow me to do so until after some cogitation, and finally I made her understand that she could not and was not allowed to remain in the body of Gottliebin. She implored me pitifully, then again acted defiantly. But I told her with a serious voice to come out of her; however, not in the Name of Jesus. I did not dare to do so for a long time. Thereupon the scene changed quickly. Gottliebin crashed down upon the bed and the possession seemed to be over.

Several days later, the seeming possession was repeated, although I did not get involved in another conversation. Soon it appeared that in this described manner three, then seven, and finally fourteen demons came out. Gottliebin's face changed each time and assumed a new threatening expression toward me. Also, many threatening words were spoken against me, to which I did not pay attention. Those present, even the mayor, received many a knock and fist-blow which, however, were never dared against me, as the demons expressly stated that they were not allowed to do anything against me, the pastor, even though they would have loved to. Here and there she tore her hair, threw her head against the wall and tried to hurt herself in many ways. However, with simple words I could rebuke every movement until at least she remained quiet, where upon the command to come out was obeyed by the demons.

Nevertheless, it seemed that the scenes became ever more horrible and as if my work made the whole thing only worse. What I suffered in spirit and soul at that time cannot be expressed in any words. My desire to end the whole thing became ever stronger. I could leave each time with the satisfaction that the demon powers had to obey, and the person was made completely right each time, yet it seemed as though the sinister power became stronger again and again. I felt as though it were trying to ensnare me in a labyrinth, to my own and my pastoral work's damage and ruin. All my friends advised me to leave the matter alone. But I had to think with horror of what would become of the person if I withdrew my hand from her, and how much I, if things went wrong, would stand accused before everyone as the cause of it all. I felt myself in a net out of which I could not possibly extricate myself by merely retreating, without danger to myself and others. In addition, I felt ashamed before myself and my Savior, to whom I prayed so much, and in whom I trusted so much, and who had given me so many proofs of His help — I confess it openly — to give in to the devil. "Who is the Lord?" I had to ask myself many times. And with faith in Him, who is the Lord, the words were formed in me again and again, “Forward! Forward! It has to lead to a good end, even though it will lead into the deepest depths, unless it were not true that Jesus had crushed the head of the serpent.”

After those fourteen demons had been expelled, the number climbed quickly to 175, then to 425. I cannot give a detailed description of the individual scenes, since everything happened too quickly and was too compressed together for me to remember details. After the last of those battles, quietness came for several days. But at night many figures pressed around the bed of Gottliebin, according to her statement. Also, a nurse said she had seen several figures at that time. One night, in her sleep, she felt herself suddenly seized on her neck by a burning hand which left huge burns. When the nurse (her aunt) who slept in the same room had lighted a light, she saw that large blisters, already filled with liquid, had risen all around her neck. The doctor, who came the next day, could not refrain from marveling at it. The neck did not heal until several weeks later. Besides that, she also received blows on her side or on her head day and night; or she was seized by her feet so that she would suddenly fall down, either on the street, or on the staircase, or wherever it might be. This resulted in bruises and other injuries. The most difficult night I had was before the 25th of July, 1842. I battled from eight o’clock in the evening until four o’clock in the morning without finishing to my satisfaction, which had never happened before. I had to leave her because I had planned a trip to the children's festival in Korntal. When I returned late that night, I was told that she was in complete delirium and that now she was to be considered nearly totally insane. Whoever saw her felt great pity. She beat her chest to pieces, tore her hair out, curled herself up like a worm and seemed to be a completely lost cause. I did not visit her until the following day at eight o'clock in the morning, after I had read in the series of my daily Bible reading, not without tears and with nearly broken heart, the strange words in the Book of Jesus Sirach, chapter 2:

> "My son, if you aspire to serve the Lord, prepare yourself for an ordeal.
> Be sincere of heart, be steadfast, and do not be alarmed when disaster comes,
> Cling to him and do not leave him, so that you may be honored at the end of your days.
> Whatever happens to you, accept it, and in the uncertainties of your humble state,
> be patient, since gold is tested in the fire, and chosen men in the furnace of humiliation.
> Trust him and he will uphold you, follow a straight path and hope in him.
> You who fear the Lord, wait for his mercy; do not turn aside in case you fall."

Strengthened by these words, I returned to the suffering one. Until about eleven o'clock everything seemed to go well. However, in the afternoon I had to return, and now it continued until seven o'clock at night, but in such a way that suddenly the demons began leaving through the mouth. She lay as dead for about a quarter of an hour. I had to muster all the strength of my faith until she breathed again; all the while I could hear from the street people calling up, "Now she is dead." After many a violent twitch in the upper part of her body, she opened wide her mouth and it was as if she spewed out one demon after another. The demons always went out in groups, mostly fourteen or twenty-eight each, or twelve each, and so they seemed to go into the thousands without a word from me. Nor did the demons say a word, except that they, when a new group came out, cast about angry looks. Finally it stopped. Now a significant period seemed to have begun. For several weeks nothing worth mentioning happened. I was glad during that time. I would never have guessed what was to follow.

4

After a period of rest, the patient came to me, pale and disfigured in countenance, to tell me something which she had kept from me until now out of shyness, but which she could no longer keep secret. She hesitated for a while, and I was anxiously wondering until finally she began telling me the following: for the last two years she had been tortured by spirit-like figures every Wednesday and Friday until she had painful and strong hemorrhages. Usually the plague of this sexual assault had lasted three hours, and she had suffered inexpressible pains through it. She had told the doctor of these hemorrhages. He had tried all sorts of medical means without being able to bring about her healing. The plague had stopped the day I had seriously taken her into consideration for the first time. But since those last days of battle (the 25th and 26th of July) it had started again. On the days mentioned she always had to go to bed in horror, and when the plague came on her, she could only groan, unable to move even the slightest bit. If this plague did not stop, she said, it would be her death. One could clearly see that she was becoming more emaciated every day during that time.

Of course, this thing frightened me considerably since I had never heard anything like it. I had only heard some vampire fairy tales which have been told in horrible, adventurous ways by writers full of fantasy. Later, of course, I heard of all sorts of tales which are current among the common people, especially that children are subject to such plagues, which are ascribed to so-called bad people; that is, witches. For the time being I needed a good bit of time to collect myself and to come to the conclusion that darkness had really received so much power over men. My next thought was, "Now you are finished. Now you go into witchcraft and magic, and what will you do against these?" But when I looked at the wailing girl, I had a horror of the possibility of the existence of that darkness and of the impossibility of help. I remembered that there were people to whom were ascribed secret arts for the defense against all sorts of demonic evils, and spiritistic remedies to which are done homage by high and low alike. Was I really to look for such things? That would mean, as I had long ago become convinced, to drive out the devil by the devil. And soon I remembered the warning I was given. I had received it already once when I was considering pinning the Name of Jesus on the door of the patient's apartment, or doing something like that, since it was often difficult to get good advice. In such thoughts, I read the reading of the community of brethren for that day, which read, "Are ye so foolish? Having begun in the Spirit, are ye now made perfect by the flesh?" (Gal. 3:3) I understood the hint and praised God, Who has always led me to stay with the honest weapons of prayer and the Word of God. "Should not," so the thought went through me, "believing prayer be able to prevail against the power of Satan, no matter what it consisted of? What should we poor little men do if no direct help could be implored from above? If Satan is in this, is it right to leave him in it? Can this not be trampled down through faith in the true God? If Jesus has come to destroy the works of the devil, should not such a thing as this be especially arrested? If there is witchcraft and magic, isn't it sin to let them go as they please without touching them, when there is the possibility of seriously going against them?" With such thoughts I worked myself into faith in the power of prayer, even in this matter in which there was no other advice left, and called out to the patient, "We shall pray, come what may. We'll try it. We can lose nothing by prayer, and the Scriptures point us to prayer and answers to prayer on nearly every page. The Lord will do what He promises." Thus I dismissed her with the assurance that I would pray for her and with the instruction to report to me again. That dreadful Friday was the following day. It was the day on which, after a drought of several months, the first thunderstorm appeared in the sky - an unforgettable day for me. When the patient walked through the door of her cousin's house, at six o'clock in the evening, the figures, as she told it, fell on her. Strong hemorrhages began. She rushed to her own home to change her clothes, and while she was sitting on a chair there, it seemed to her as if she had to swallow something continually. After a few moments this caused her to be beside herself. She rushed like mad through both rooms and heatedly demanded a knife. Her frightened brother and sister would not allow a knife to get into her hands. Then she ran to the attic, jumped on the window sill and already stood outside the window in free air, only holding on with one hand on the in side, when the first flash of lightning of the approaching thunderstorm met her eye, then frightened, and awakened her. She came to and cried, "For God's sake, I don't want to do that." The moment of light disappeared, and in the returning delirium she took hold of a rope (where she got it, she cannot explain to this day) and tied it skillfully around the beams of the attic. She made a noose which easily pulled tight. She had nearly forced her whole head into the noose, when a second flash of lightning caught her eye through the window. As before, it brought her back to consciousness. A stream of tears flowed from her eyes the following day when she looked at the noose hanging from the beam. She could never have tied it as skillfully in the best of consciousness. Then she remained somewhat awake and crawled the short distance to her cousin's house. She was extremely exhausted from the continuing hemorrhages. All she could do was to get up the stairs to the chamber in the attic where she slept at that time. She fell unconscious into her bed. Then I was called. The thunderstorm had already begun. It was toward eight o'clock at night. I found her swimming in blood which forced itself through her dress everywhere on the upper part of her body. The first words of consolation which I called out to her had the effect that she came to a little and cried, "Oh, the figures." "Do you see them?" I asked.

The answer was a wailing groan. Then I began to pray seriously, while the thunder rolled outside. What I said, I do not know anymore. But the effect after a quarter of an hour was so decisive that she called out, "Now they are gone." Soon she came to completely, and I went out for a few moments until she had changed her dress. There was only praise and gratitude among us when we saw her so totally changed, sitting on her bed. From that day on the above- mentioned plague ceased. Only a few times afterwards did she still see figures as if trying to fall upon her. However, besides that nothing occurred again, until this, too, stopped. Whatever the matter was, she was helped.

However, the work of that night was not over by any means. While we were still standing around and singing songs of praise, the patient sank backwards as usual when demonic attacks came on her. Wrathful words of threatening came out, which I could easily command to cease. Then she seemingly returned to consciousness.

"You can go now," she said.

"But can I be at rest?" I replied.

"Why not?" she continued. "You don't trust me at all."

"Is that right?" I said. "No, I don't trust you at all."

With these remarks, I laid aside my hat and cane. While I prayed a short prayer, the demon broke out of her with sneering laughter and said, "You did the right thing that you did not leave. You would have lost and lost all." I did not pay much attention to what was said and acted and spoke in the usual way. Suddenly the wrath and ill humor of the demons broke loose with full strength, and many statements like the following were heard, mostly in a howling and wailing voice: "Now everything is lost! Now everything is betrayed! You disturb us thoroughly. The whole alliance goes to pieces. All is over. Everything is confusion. It is your fault with your constant praying. Woe, woe. You will yet drive us out. All is lost. We are 1,067, and those who are still alive are many, too." Of those who were still alive, they said, "One should warn them. Woe to them, woe; they are lost."

At this point I interjected, "Those who are still alive can be converted. God may still save them. You better think of yourselves." But I was answered with a strong voice, "They have signed themselves over by blood."

"To whom?"

"To the devil, to the devil."

Of such blood contract much was said later, especially with the epithet, "Sworn against God, lost forever," as if the people who had sworn themselves to the devil were not able to be converted and saved anymore. However, they seemed to say that more about themselves, who had died. At the present moment, the demons showed nothing but despair, because they were sure that their way led into the abyss. The roaring of the demons, the flashing of the lightning bolts, the rolling thunder, the splashing of the downpour, the seriousness of those present, the prayers I prayed, upon which the demons came out in the way previously mentioned — all of that made a scene no one could imagine in any way corresponding to reality.

After a few hours, however, everything became quiet, and I left the patient with more joy than ever. I could already convince myself that the battle in which I stood was a very special one, of whose special meaning I already had seen some light, but which did not become completely clear until later. By the way, when the demons said, among other things, "No one in the world would have driven us out, only you with your constant prayer and perseverance are seeing this through," it was not quite inexplicable to me. For no one would easily have given himself in such a way as I. And certainly not those who, and I am honest enough to write down such statements too, would accuse me of proud self-glorification.

5

What I related last, happened in August of 1842. During the course of the following days it became evident that by far not all the demons had been removed from the patient. The time spent in this case seemed to be very long to me now, especially since I was pressed for time because of much work to which I had promised myself besides my ministry. A faithful friend in a neighboring state, to whom in that time I had the opportunity and courage to tell my difficult position, finally pointed me to the word, “This kind goeth not out but by prayer and fasting.” (Matthew 17:21) And when I thought more upon this, I came to the point of giving more importance to fasting than one usually does. Fasting is an actual proof before God that the matter of prayer is a true and urgent one to the believer. It reinforces the intention and strength of prayer to a high degree. It even represents a continual prayer with out words. Because of this, I could believe that it would have effect, especially since in the case in which I stood, I had a special word from the Lord. I tried fasting without telling anyone about it. I must confess that the following battles were made extraordinarily easier because of it. I especially gained from the fact that I could talk much more quietly, firmly and with determination, and did not have to spend as much time as before. I felt that I could, without being present, have a strong effect upon the case. When I came, I realized great results in a few moments. That was especially the case after the attack in August when the patient felt more strongly that a demon of the worst kind was in her. She would often lie as dead while her breath was held from within her. She was also stabbed and pressed in many ways internally. Also, sometimes, she was so paralyzed that she could hardly move a member of her body by her own will. During that time she was extremely bad-tempered and repellent, and visits by me became particularly adverse to her. But the worst was that again blood was forced from the inside against the outer skin, as with pricking instruments. Hemorrhages began anew, although the cause seemed to be a different one from before. I fasted, but found circumstances worse than ever on that day. However, through prayer the hemorrhages stopped. But the demon spoke so defiantly, mockingly, and blasphemously through her, that I remained completely quiet and made ready to leave, trusting in the power of silent prayer. Then the demon tried to stop me from leaving, but obviously in such a way as to make fun of me. I left. Whatever raged and raved in Gottliebin, even though I was called by someone out of fear for the life of the patient, I did not allow myself to visit her again that day. And in reality, the power of the demon broke during the following night, and on the third day it fled from my side nearly without a word, although not without having almost totally burned her throat. This caused her pain and much trouble for a long time.

6

I can no longer give a coherent story until February of 1843. I only remember that I felt a constant burden and need, although always sustained by the hope that finally the end would come. Therefore, I add several general remarks here, although I admit with fearless openness, that all sorts of considerations advise me to be reticent. It turned out more and more that a great change had taken place with the demons which had come to the forefront. There were many of them which had returned several times, but returned no more. Nevertheless, Gottliebin saw me swarmed round about in a terrible way by demons when I was in church, standing in the pulpit. It seemed as though all of them tried to do me harm. I cannot say that I did not feel their effect, even during the time when I did not know this yet, for Gottliebin had held it back from me for a long time out of consideration for me. But neither can I say that the effect was so strong that it would prove the statements of Gottliebin. Especially in my sermons, I felt more strengthened than weakened. That is why I cannot say anything definite. With other spirits which identified themselves from then on, there seemed to be a question of what was going to happen to them. It was peculiar that from the beginning Gottliebin was constantly in the company of these demons, either in her sleep or when she was not in her right mind. She knew many of them but did not know anything about

that which occurred between the demons and me. Furthermore, she always saw the demons which were driven out for some time after in the room, especially the last one, which appeared as the head over many. It always appeared with an immense book, into which it reportedly wrote the names of all those subject to it. Gottliebin perceived it in a peculiarly bordered and expensive garment which pointed to a very ancient time. The demons themselves appeared quite different to Gottliebin in reference to their character. Some of them she always found full of wrath and rage, and always in deliberations as to how to protect themselves against attacks made against them through the Word of God. The others seemed to be held by force by the former. The difference could be noted also in those demons which spoke out of her. Some were defiant, full of hatred against me, and often spoke words which were worthy of being recorded. They had a terror of the abyss, which they felt near now, and said, among other things, "You are our worst enemy, but we, too, are your enemies. If only we could as we would!" And then again, "Oh, if only there were no God in heaven!"
Besides that, they ascribed all guilt for their destruction to themselves. The behavior of one demon which Gottliebin had seen before in her house, and which identified itself now as a perjurer, was horrible. It called out repeatedly these words which, were painted on a window shutter,

"O, Man, think of eternity, don't miss the
time of grace, for judgment is not far."

Then it fell silent, made a grimace and lifted up three fingers high in a stiff way, suddenly shivered and groaned. I would have liked to have had more spectators for these scenes, which occurred often. The greatest number of those demons which identified themselves between August of 1842 and February of 1843 later belonged to those which languished with a burning craving to be free from the bonds of Satan. The most varied languages with strange accents occurred, mostly such as I could not compare to any European language, except for Italian and French, according to the sound. The attempts of such demons to speak German, especially when they circumscribed concepts whose German meaning they seemed not to know, were peculiar and sometimes comical. In between I could hear words which I could not put into either of these categories of demons, but which sounded as if they came from a higher region. To that category belonged quotations, frequent beyond measure, of Habakkuk 2:3,4. "The vision is yet for an appointed time, but at the end it shall speak, and not lie: though it tarry, wait for it; because it will surely come, it will not tarry. Behold, his soul which is lifted up is not upright in him: but the just shall live by his faith." Then it was again as though the same higher voice were trying to turn to the demons by quoting a verse which I could not find for a long time, until I finally recognized it in Jeremiah 3:25. Instead of the first person "we" the second person "you" was used. "You lie down in your shame, and your confusion covers you, for you have sinned against the Lord your God, you and your fathers, from your youth even until this day, and have not obeyed the voice of the Lord your God." This and other verses from the Bible I did not understand for a long time, but slowly I learned to pay more attention to them and to see more meaning in them. In such quotations, which at times came at the end of a battle, I felt as if strength was offered me from on high. At the same time I cannot but look with the most moving gratitude upon the many preservations and deliverances which were accorded to me, amid horrid scenes, again and again. The patient was tortured incessantly. Her body would often swell extraordinarily, and she would vomit whole buckets of water. This seemed so strange to the doctor, who was always present, as one could not understand where all that water came from. She also received frequent blows on her head, knocks in the side, and in addition suffered from heavy nose bleeding, constipation, and other things. And with all the things going on in her, it seemed to be heading for a fatal turn. But through prayer and faith the attacks were made harmless and pushed back.

7

From that period I want to mention something more about the demons that yearned for liberation. For a long time I did not listen to their talk, and was often pressed upon when I saw the painful expressions of their faces, their hands lifted pleading and the streams of tears which flowed from their eyes, and heard the sounds and sighs of fear, despair and begging which could have moved a stone. I was much against talking with them about salvation because in all that was happening I always thought first of the possibility of dangerous and fatal deception of the devil, and because I feared for the sobriety of my evangelical faith. But finally I felt I had to make an attempt, especially since those very demons which seemed to have some hope for themselves, could not be dislodged either by threats or by admonitions. The first demon with which I dared to deal was, as far as I remember, the woman through whom the whole thing got started. She showed herself again in Gottliebin and cried with a firm and decided voice that she wanted to belong to the Savior and not to the devil. Then she said how much had been changed in the world of spirits through these battles up to now. She said that my good fortune had been that I had remained solely with the Word of God and prayer. If I had tried anything else and even taken refuge in secretly working means, as they were frequently used among the common people, and to which the demons had tempted me, I would have been lost. She said this to me with an ominously raised finger and concluded with the words, "That was a horrible battle which you have undertaken." Then she begged and implored me that I might pray for her so that she would get completely free from the power of the devil, into which she had come nearly ignorantly through idolatry, spiritism, and magic; and to pray that she might find a place of rest somewhere. I had known that woman well during her lifetime, and she had shown a desire for the Word of God and for consolations I had not seen easily in others. Hardly a week passed that she did not come twice or thrice to my house to visit me. She had especially desired the song, "Rest is the best possession," from me. Now my heart wanted to break for her and looking to the Lord in my heart, I asked her, "Where do you want to go?"

"I want to stay in your house," she responded.

I was frightened and said, "That can never be."

"Can't I go into the church?" she continued.

I thought a while and then said, "If you promise me that you won't make yourself visible and won't disturb anybody, and under the condition that Jesus gives you permission, I have nothing against it."

It was a risky undertaking on my part, but I relied on the Lord that he would make everything right. I did not feel I had gone into presumption before Him. She seemed contented, mentioned the farthest corner where she would go and then went out, easily and of her own accord, as it seemed. Nothing of all this was told the patient, and yet to her great horror, she saw the woman at the designated place in the church. But no one besides her noticed anything about this, and after a while the whole appearance ceased. On the whole, everything kept changing throughout the following battles. In similar ways other spirits tried to find freedom and security, spirits which pretended to be still bound to the devil because of idolatry and magic, but otherwise to have love for the Savior. Only with the utmost caution and earnest prayer to the Lord did I get involved in the unavoidable. My main word always was, "If Jesus permits it." I could see that divine guidance was in this. Not all obtained what they longed for, and many had to go out relying on the free mercy of the Lord. I do not wish to enlarge upon this subtle point and only want to mention that no disturbance was caused while the patient was constantly alleviated. Such spirits which are given a temporary place of rest must not be confused with real evil spirits. The latter always appear under the judgment and under the power of Satan, of which others are free. I could make many comments about what I experienced, but I would rather keep them to myself as they could only cause stumbling. Furthermore, since they are not founded on the Bible, they do not deserve further attention. There is only one very interesting case I cannot omit. One of the spirits also asked to be allowed into the church. I said my usual, "If Jesus permits." After a while it broke out into a desperate crying and called, or heard someone call, "God is a judge of widows and orphans." A further comment was that it was not allowed to go into the church. I said, "You see that it is the Lord who shows you the way and that it is not I who decide this. Go where the Lord commands you to go." Then it continued, "Could I perhaps go into your house?" This request surprised me, and thinking of my wife and children, I was not inclined to allow this. But then I thought, "Maybe this is a temptation for me to show that I would be willing to suffer every sacrifice," and therefore I finally said, "If you don't disquiet anyone and Jesus allows you to, then let it be." Suddenly I heard something else again, as from a voice on high, calling out of the mouth of the patient, "Not under a roof! God is a judge of widows and orphans." The spirit again began crying, as it appeared, and asked that at least it be allowed to go into my garden, which it now seemed to be permitted to do. It was as if at one time orphans had lost their home because of it. In this fashion it continued for a while. Whatever spirit was given a resting place did not return again. Many identified themselves by formally giving their names, which was done especially by those who had died since I had been installed as pastor in this town. Others mentioned the place where they were from, often hundreds of hours away. Some even said they came from America. I left these things undecided as to how far I had to take them as true, and was just happy to get rid of them. I do want to add to this that neither the dogma of purgatory nor the dogma of prayer for the dead are confirmed by the above in any way. The latter is so dangerous that I do want to warn every man of it in all seriousness. The most devastating effects from the unseen world can be the consequence of it.

There is something else that, in summarizing, I have to report. This will call for attention, but I cannot be silent about it by any means. Through the above appearances, and others later, I realized that our time suffers from an evil that has eaten through nearly the entire evangelical Christendom like a secretly gnawing worm. No one is paying serious attention to it. And that is the sin of idolatry, which by steps leads up to magic and complete black magic. I received the surest knowledge of its existence in a most horrible way. Idolatry may be considered every reliance on a supernatural, invisible power, based upon which a man is attempting to obtain either health, honor, gain or pleasure, as long as this power is not purely divine. But every superstitious use of pious words, especially when the Highest Names are used in it, is also idolatry, because the living faith in God, as well as the highness and majesty of God are made into a caricature. In this category belongs every kind of spiritism whose effectiveness has lately been recognized more decisively than ever before by high and low. Therefore, it is being used thoughtlessly by everybody, at least in its seemingly innocent sphere. People do not think what apostasy from God such thoughtless degradation of the Name and Power of God presupposes; nor do they think what an apostasy from God the invisibly working power in such cases really is and alone can be. Due to this and many other things which I pass over here, man gets hung up on an immediate natural power. He changes his faith in the invisible God to a kind of nature spirit. Because of it he becomes an idolater in the eyes of the jealous God, for God does not give His glory to another, as the Old Testament says. If an immediate, invisible power is to help, why does not man turn to Him Who Himself is Power?

Even less to be excluded from the sphere of idolatry is the so-called transplantation. It is an art by which pain or disease are attempted to be transferred into trees or animals by all sorts of manipulations.

Slowly I learned to get a glimpse into the horrible consequences of all this idolatry. The first effect is that a man becomes more or less bound to a sinister satanic power. This happens through a demon which wins influence over him because it is enticed through the act of idolatry. This influence may be physical and may cause every kind of nervous disorder, cramps, gout, and other diseases which doctors know little about what to do. It also may cause psychical (soulish) effects such as melancholy, depression, or gross indulgences such as lewd passions, lust, drunkenness, stinginess, envy, wrath, vengeance, and other passions which often become such a burden to man that he cannot master them. What Paul writes on idolatry in his epistle to the Romans, that they changed the glory of the eternal God into all sorts of foolishness, is literally fulfilled in our Christian idolatry. Christians put their confidence in senseless sayings, secret formulas and signs, in certain days and pieces of paper which they hang on their necks as the Africans their grigris. They also devour them and commit other horrors which would lead too far to discuss here. A further consequence is the loss of sensitivity to the Word of Truth, indifference to sin and dulling of spirit against higher emotions, thoughts and security regarding eternity. And on the other hand, no consolation will remain in the heart in times of suffering, and especially when the conscience is accused, the evangelical joy cannot take root. The saddest consequence for man comes after death, if he does not recognize the above mentioned idolatry and repent of it before death. That is what I experienced in my battles with horrors, until I was convinced in many ways. The bond with which he tied himself to the dark power is not loosed. The person, who a moment ago thought himself to be ready for the joys of heaven, is held as an apostate by the enemy. And according to his predicament, he is forced against his will to serve the devil for the torture of the living. I refrain from speaking about this realm anymore since it is difficult and risky to speak about such mysterious matters with any degree of certainty.

8

After many experiences, the 8th of February of 1843 neared. Gottliebin lay on her bed nearly all day, unconscious, but without causing us concern. It seemed that she was granted a rest, but a rest which had to be considered more as a being caught away in her spirit into far regions. I report it as she told it to me afterwards. It seemed to her that someone led her with extraordinary speed over land and sea. She was floating above the surface. She flew through many countries and cities, passed over ships in the ocean whose crews she could clearly see and hear talk until she came to a world of islands. She floated from island to island. Finally she came to a high mountain on whose pinnacle she was set down. On the summit was a large, wide opening out of which spewed fire and smoke. All around her lightning flashed, thunder rolled, and the earth quaked. In the coastal areas at the foot of the mountains she saw that cities and villages were overthrown, and the dust rose up high. On the ocean, ships and other conveyances went into confusion, and many of them sank into the water. In the middle of this scene of horror the demons which had tortured her most up until then were brought forth. The worst of all, the same demon with the immense book, was the first which was cast headlong into the abyss with great roaring and screaming. After him about a thousand others followed, all of whom rushed upon Gottliebin as if to try to drag her with them into the abyss. When all of this was over, Gottliebin was brought back in the same way as she had gone there and awakened, rather terrified, but otherwise well. I cannot guarantee what she told here, but I was astonished and surprised above measure when a short time later newspapers reported in detail about the terrible earthquake which happened exactly on the 8th of February in the West Indies. The descriptions of the community of brethren, especially those which I read in the missions class, transported Gottliebin completely back into that which she had seen in her spirit. From that time on she did not see me swarmed about by spirits in the church any more. Two more such raptures occurred in the following days, but in such a way that she seemed to float over Asia. I cannot keep silent about what relationship the earthquake of that time had with the battle here, or with the weather and other things. The drought of the year 1842 and the excess of rain of the year 1843 were mentioned by the demons. The thing that horrified me the most was that the many fires in cities (the demons put the number at thirty-six) were directly related to the influence, even the direct work of the demons. One demon especially came to the fore, which pretended to have fanned the flames of Hamburg with special ravenous lust. I asked him what had caused him to do this. He answered with one word, "Lust". On the other hand it was indicated that Satan, noticing that he was being robbed of many tools of magic, was intent on plunging thousands into disaster in order to recruit new victims who would be easily moved to sell themselves to the devil with blood. Once it was added, "He has succeeded." It was terrifying to listen to the frequent threats of the demons to set fire to our whole town and especially to my house. Often they sneered at me in a ghastly way and said, "Blood or fire!" It struck me, that once in an especially hard night of battle, a herd of sheep was brought into fear and confusion by an unknown dog over which the shepherd could not gain the mastery. The following morning two of the largest sheep lay torn under my window. I mention this because once the demons said, "Blood, even if it is only a sheep."

9

Even though up to now I have told unheard of and incomprehensible things, the worst is still before me. I will honestly continue telling what I remember, convinced that the Lord will have His hand over me in this report. My only desire is to tell everything to the glory of Him who is Victor over all the powers of darkness.

On the 8th of February a new period began in the history of Gottliebin's possession. From then on even more definite forms and effects of the most varied magic came to my observation. I was aghast to realize that everything which thus far had been held among the most ridiculous popular beliefs stepped out of the world of fairy tales into reality. First, I will summarize all the appearances in the area of magic which occurred during the course of the year 1843.

It was shown that things without number in the body of Gottliebin had been, to use the only word possible, charmed into her body, all with the intent to put her out of this world. It started with vomiting up sand and small pieces of glass. After a while all sorts of pieces of iron came out, especially old and bent board nails. Once, after much retching, twelve of these fell into the bowl held under her, right before my eyes. Gottliebin also vomited shoe buckles of varied sizes and forms, often so large that one could hardly understand how they could even come up her throat. Once an especially large and broad piece of iron came, at which her breath stopped and she lay as dead for several minutes. Besides those, an uncountable amount of pins, needles, and pieces of knitting needles came out, often single, when the going was the hardest, and often in masses, tied together with feathers and paper. Often it looked as though the knitting needles had been drawn across through her head, from one ear to the other, and once several finger-long pieces came out at the ear. At another occasion, when I was laying on hands, I could feel how the needles broke in the head or turned and bent together. Those were steel needles, which then slowly eased their way towards the throat and came out at the mouth. These iron needles could be bent and finally, bent three or four times but whole, found their way out of the mouth. I also pulled many pins out of the nose which had eased their way down from above, the points heading down. I had first felt them lying across over the nose-bone. Once fifteen of these pins came out of her nose with such violence that all of them got stuck in Gottliebin's hand which she had held to her nose. At another time she complained much of a headache and when I laid on hands, I saw white points shimmering everywhere. There were twelve pins which were still half in her head and which I pulled out one by one while she showed her pains by jerking each time. Once I pulled two, then again four pins, out of her eye, which moved around under her eyelids for a long time until they came out a little so that they could be pulled out with care. Furthermore, I pulled a lot of needles out of all parts of the upper and lower jaws. At first she would feel terrific pains in her teeth, but nothing could be seen for a long time until finally the points could be felt. Then as they came out more and more and I could finally take hold of them, much strength was still needed to pull them out all the way. Two old finger-long pieces of wire showed themselves in the tongue and it cost time and pains until they were taken out completely. Two long, bent pieces of wire were wrapped around her womb under the skin. My wife and I needed about an hour until they had all come out, while Gottliebin fainted more than once, which, by the way, happened many times. In addition, whole knitting needles, and halves, came so frequently and at different times out of all parts of her upper body, that I estimate there were at least thirty. Sometimes they came out crooked, sometimes straight, in the latter case especially out of her pericardium. Often when the needles were already half out, I still had to do about half an hour of pulling with all my strength. Also other things, such as needles of all lengths, large pieces of glass, small stones, and once a long piece of iron came out of the upper part of her body.

I cannot really think it wrong if anybody is suspicious of the above report, since everything goes beyond all we can think or understand. But the continuous observations and experiences of nearly one whole year allow me to tell these things freely and boldly. I always had several eyewitnesses with me. I insisted upon this without fail in order to prevent evil rumors. I am completely sure, which I have to be in regard to Gottliebin's character, that not the least fraud occurred nor could occur. However often I visited her during that time, called or uncalled, there was always something moving around. And after a while an object of magic would work its way out of her body. Each time the pain was so terrific that she would more or less lose consciousness. Usually she would say, "I cannot stand this; this is my death." But everything could be brought out only through prayer. When she began to complain that she had pains somewhere, I had only to lay on hands, usually on her head, and because I was exercised in the faith through long experience, I was sure that I would experience the power of prayer, which I spoke with few words. Then she would begin to feel the thing start moving or turning, trying to find an exit. The most difficult part was through the outer skin. Often one could feel for a long time how something was pressing from the inside to the outside. Blood never flowed, nor was a wound caused. The most one could see for a while was the spot where some object had worked itself out, but only if it was taken out by prayer. Sometimes, however, she would cut her skin and be overwhelmed by the pain when I was not there. These wounds could hardly ever be healed. There were so many objects that I could not enumerate them all. The only other thing I will mention is that even living animals came out of her mouth, but

I never had opportunity to see them. Once four of the largest locusts came out, and were taken alive to a meadow where they quickly jumped away. At another time, six to eight bats, one of which was beaten to death, came out. The others fled quickly. At still another time a friend of hers pulled out of her throat an immensely large frog. Finally, Gottliebin saw briefly a mysterious serpent of the adder family, and of the most dangerous kind, come out, but no one else saw it. Yet, I did think I had seen a quickly moving shimmering streak gliding from her mouth over the bed. This adder caused her a wound on her neck soon after it had come out of her mouth, and at another time it stung her so violently on her foot while she was sitting at the table with the family, that the bleeding nearly did not stop. Both wounds caused her much pain for several months, and it could clearly be seen that they were dangerous, poisonous wounds.

I cannot close this part of the account of the battle without at least telling of one case of the most hideous kind in more detail. At the beginning of December of 1843, Gottliebin had a case of nose bleeding which just wouldn't stop. When she had just lost a bowl of blood, it started all over again. It is inconceivable how her life could be maintained with such an immense loss of blood. The striking thing was that the blood always had a pungent smell and looked especially black. The reason for that was the magic of poisoning, of which we will speak later. The doctor visited her in this need and prescribed something, but hardly had any hope himself that the medication would have any effect. Then at one o'clock in the afternoon, on a walk to the branch church that took me past her house, I visited her. She had just changed her clothes and was sitting in a chair, exhausted. Also the living room had just been cleaned of blood which had flowed freely in the morning. She showed me several spots on her head and said that something was in there, and if it did not come out, she would have to die. I could not feel anything special and told her that I would not see her until after my return, because I was in a hurry. After me, Dr. Späth, the doctor, came. He remained with her for two hours and had her tell him a lot of things. He, too, could feel something hard at the places mentioned. He sensed that something was going to happen and wanted to wait until it was over, but he was suddenly called to a childbirth in Simozheim. Around four o'clock I was nearing the town again, when a messenger rushed toward me and said I was to hurry to Gottliebin. I sped there, and to my horror I could see the people everywhere looking out of their windows and crying to me, "Pastor, there is a great need." I entered. A suffocating vapor of blood almost drove me out again. Gottliebin sat in the middle of the small living room, with a bucket in front of her which was about half filled with blood and water. The whole length of the living room behind and in front of her was covered with blood. She herself was completely covered with blood, so that one could hardly recognize her clothing. Just think, blood running quickly out of both of her ears, both of her eyes and her nose and even out of the upper part of her head. That was the most gruesome thing I have ever seen. A number of people had seen it through the window but were afraid to remain. At first I did not know what to do, but I collected my self and after a short, serious sigh of prayer the bleeding stopped for the time being. She could not be recognized any more and I had someone wash her face and her head. Then I touched the place on her head where something was supposed to be. On the front part of her head above the forehead, I noticed something, and soon a small, bent nail bored itself through. At the back part of her head something turned and worked itself down, and finally a bent board nail came out. But from then on the bleeding stopped. The first faint into which she fell when I entered was overcome, as well as others which followed. In the evening she felt rather well and strengthened again. All the other things I could tell if I had had time to write a diary!

10

During the many battles which I had to go through after the one just mentioned, I thought a great deal about the way and manner in which the magic powers were used. I felt a need to be able to think at least of some explanation for myself. Of course, I thought that there are still secrets about the essence of matter which philosophy has not found out with surety. I thought if matter were a conglomeration of a kind of atoms, as already many philosophers thought, then magic would be, I supposed, nothing else but a secret art taught by the sinister power: how to dissolve the bonds between the different atoms in order to make the object which is being used unrecognizable, even invisible. Then it enters with other things; for example, ordinary food, where the person who exercises this art wants it to go. Then the dissolved bonds are reestablished there, and the object appears the same as it was before. Thus Gottliebin could well remember from former times that once in a while she would immediately feel something strange in her throat or in her body after having eaten a soup or other dishes. Once she tossed a leftover of such a meal to a chicken. Immediately the chicken ran around like mad and after a while fell over dead, as if suffocated. She opened the neck and head of the chicken and to her horror there were a lot of shoe nails. But how could other things get into her head and body and the upper part of her body? What Gottliebin had to tell was enlightening. At night she had often seen in her spirit persons of all kinds and social levels come to the side of her bed. While she was always lying motionless, they would give her something like bread, put it into her mouth or touch other parts of her body and soon she would feel a change in her which coincided with the objects which came out later. That board nail and the smaller nail which caused the heavy bleeding were put into her head by a special manipulation at night in the middle of the street. Someone was waiting for her there, not physically, but rather in the spirit, as she thought. He wore an ornate priestly garment. She could not offer the least resistance. Soon after that the bleeding began. Once three men came in front of her in the same way: that is to say, as spirits, and held a poisonous fluid in their hand. Again she could not move. One of them opened her mouth, the other held her head, and the third wanted to pour the fluid in. A little of it went into her mouth and in order to suffocate her, her jaws were pressed shut. But the vapor of the fluid went out through her nose, and since she could at least sigh, she was saved. When the men noticed that they could not do anything, they poured the contents of the glass over her head and left. The next morning her night cap was completely eaten by a yellow, evil smelling substance, and upon touch fell apart easily. At another time when she was sleeping in her own room, she had hung her dress on the door of the bedroom, and her sister, who was sleeping in the same bed with her, knew for sure what was in the pocket of that dress, and also that Gottliebin had not left the bed. But at night Gottliebin saw a figure go to her dress, take out a tin money box of the kind farmers use, beside other things. Then it stepped in front of her with these things. And on the following morning, she vomited pieces of money and the tin money box with violent retching. This all leads up to the fact that there are people who have the art of being outside of their bodies, in the spirit, probably not always while completely conscious. But to charm objects into the inside of the body: how can this be? The fact which gives light on this matter was that always someone deceased or a demon worked with all the objects which were charmed into her body. It alone exercised the art and entered into the person with the object. And in this way it was represented many times. That is why possession was evident really only because of magic. The case was not that of the cure of a possessed woman, but of the liberation of a person charmed by magic. The fact that the objects did not actually kill her, as was the intention of the darkness, is due to a special preservation by God. This showed itself in a marked way as soon as the spell began, because Gottliebin hardly felt the objects within her until the time had come for them to be removed. Some of those things must have been in her for more than two years. So to speak, a demon was always the guardian of these objects. Because of that the magic spell was not brought into motion until I was present or more especially when I was moved to pray for her, even while absent. It was the rule, therefore, that either after or before the removal of the charm, a demon went out. One firm conviction I have is that Gottliebin would have been lost if even once I had given in to unbelief, as if it were not possible to do the seemingly impossible through prayer alone. But I always felt so strengthened that I believed my Savior could do anything. And the thought that took greater hold of me every day, was that through this battle a severe blow must be dealt to the black art of magic, and it made me endure the uttermost.

What I just said was the result of many observations, experiences, and constant reflection upon the strange appearances. I cannot but set forth in greater detail the conclusions which I drew slowly, and which allowed me to look into the nature and essence of magic with considerable surety. Accordingly, in order to effect a charm, a dead and a living person cooperated. It can happen through the formerly mentioned idolatries, and unfortunately does happen to a horrible degree, that a man without knowing it and without noticing it, is bound in spirit by Satan. His spirit, of course a psychological mystery, can be absent from the body even though the soul, as it seems, is present in the body. In the spirit he is brought into connection and communion with other equally bound people, as well as with the dead, who also had bound themselves more or less during their lifetime. It is really the latter who exercise magic, while the former serve to provide the materials. According to many a remark of the demons, the living who are bound to Satan through spiritualism as well as by bold curses, through gross sins of the flesh, etc., must serve him against their will, in their spirit, although this compulsion varies according to the degree of the sin of idolatry indulged in. Finally, I myself was led to the conclusion to think of a certain satanic plot according to which all of mankind was to be drawn away after the plan of the devil, slowly, unawares, and with deception, in order for the reign of Satan to become more common and the reign of Christ to be destroyed. In this undertaking the sinister power had the greater fortune, since everything happened in the greatest secrecy. Wherever something came to the fore and was noticed, nobody was even thinking in the least to go against it with courage and faith. Most of the witches and warlocks to whom are ascribed all kinds of misfortune, disease, plagues of men and cattle, are what they are in this capacity, without their knowledge. The most would be that once in a while they have a feeling of what they do in the spirit without being able to explain this feeling. In any case, they are highly unfortunate people, and from this follows that the accusation of a living person is unmerciful as a rule and must be rejected to begin with. It cannot lead to any result, because the accused are often completely innocent. If not always, at least as a rule, they consider themselves innocent, even though they are forced to make a confession through instruments of torture as in witch trials. I thank God that from the very beginning I started with the premise not to allow any accusation for which I would often have had cause and never to judge someone based on their outward appearance. I would have gotten into horrible confusion through this, and Satan would easily have won against me and my work. If, however, the bound person in his normal life is not conscious of what he does in the spirit or is forced to do, it cannot be concluded that he is not accountable. He is accountable for the very reason that the basis of his bound condition is the sin of idolatry. In addition, even in the spirit he retains his free will to give himself over to Satan completely or not. All accountability and consequences will disappear, however, if only the idolatry indulged in is confessed and repented of, since it is one of the most severe sins. It goes directly against the first commandment and embodies the very apostasy from God. The sins of idolatry must be repented of during one's lifetime; otherwise, the bound condition goes on after death. This repentance, however, does not happen usually for the following reasons: first, one does not fear any danger from idolatry; second, one does not recognize the danger of it even though one has an inexplicable horror of it; and third, one does not estimate the danger as being high enough. Now the eyes of the person who was deceived and caught in the snare of the devil, are opened. But even now he still has the free will to decide whether he wants to give himself over completely to the devil's service or not. In the former case he becomes a regular magic spirit who is now commanded by Satan, together with other living magicians, to torture these people in various ways, either in their bodies, or their cattle, or in other ways. The purpose of these plagues is none other than to drive these people into a corner so that they in turn will also use superstitious and idolatrous means in order to be caught in the snare themselves. Therefore, many misfortunes which come upon man are really trials of Job, allowed by God in order to show whether man will bless God for them or not. Oh, how carelessly man lives and acts for the moment! The magic of the living has, by the way, a series of steps. On the lowest level are those who, as the saying goes, are being used in magic itself, and thus become ensnared without being conscious of it from then on. The highest level is black magic proper, in which the person serves Satan with full consciousness and who is granted these powers by him. In the middle between the two categories are those who make a trade out of the use of magic and who are being used and fetched by people for this purpose. Usually they use printed booklets, of which many are being circulated among the common people, and which are revelations of Satan proper. They also work according to tradition. This third category of magicians can speak their formulas and do their manipulations for a long time with the seeming consciousness of being benefactors of mankind, even in the reputation of great piety, although always with a bad conscience. But they are being ensnared deeper and deeper through their heathen practices, and therefore the danger of becoming black magicians proper comes closer and closer. Closest, although probably still deceived, are those who receive, if I may say so, demons from the devil, which become their counselors and through which the magicians inquire. These demons appear to them, either visibly or invisibly, through certain means which they use, including mirrors. The demons answer the questions asked of them, of course not without an interest in the reign of darkness. Thus it comes that Christians ask advice at the mouth of Beezlebub (2. Kings 1). Black magicians proper are those who, so to speak, have made a formal pact with the devil. This can happen individually or through joining certain societies, the foundation of which is such a secret pact. In both cases the signing of the name with blood takes place. This is done by cutting the finger or some other part of the body and using the blood which flows to sign one's name. If the signing is done individually, it can either be done through a formal pact with the devil, of which, however, that person does not always retain consciousness, or in the spirit, in which case that person does not retain consciousness either. What black magicians are looking for mostly is good fortune, lust, money, and protection against bodily dangers. The arts they possess are of many kinds. They are able to provide money for themselves, make themselves invisible, in the same way in which the before mentioned objects are made invisible, move hundreds of miles in a few moments, and that with their whole personage. Especially, they can kill people hundreds of hours away, and strokes of which often the healthiest persons die can be the consequence of a magic stroke from a shorter or longer distance. They also start fires without being seen. Of course, I have to leave everyone to himself as to what he wants to believe of these things. But alas, the horrible surety I gained of their existence! However, a battle against these sinister powers, begun by faith in Him who crushed the head of the serpent, could never but be victorious. Our Lord is still greater!

11

The above remarks are partially founded on facts which occurred during my battle with the devil and partially on interspersed, incoherent remarks of those demons which seemingly seek liberation or had found it, and partially through other psychological observations which I had sufficient opportunity to make once my eyes had been opened to these things. One might perhaps accuse me of having gone too much after these things and of having allowed a dreamer's fantasy to rule. But I really did not have any time for fantastic meditations. Just think, the above-mentioned battles lasted for nearly two years and took a high toll of time and soul, going on at the same time as my ministry, to which I always gave all of my attention with all my love, especially during the last years. As the pastor's reports show, I undertook much in the mother church as well as in the daughter church in order to have a teaching and an awakening effect upon my community. During the whole time I was busy as a writer. I wrote monthly publications for public missionary meetings and provided articles for Barth's youth magazine, such as, "On the Appearance and Effects of Light." Furthermore, a small book of world history and another on the history of missions and mission geography were completed. The latter of which, as far as I had moments to spare, buried me in mountains of German, English and French mission publications, and it is just now leaving the press. Nor could I remain passive when there was such an active stirring in our fatherland for the new hymnal and the new liturgy. Once, even twice, I supplied an extensive plan for a new chorale book for which I searched and gathered with much effort old chorales and melodies in many old writings. In order to awaken new interest for the chorale, I had a collection printed. For this purpose, I first had to acquaint myself with the theory of music. Beside this, I held a double teaching conference last summer as the director of the school conference, one on the treatment of the German language in elementary schools and the other on the life of the apostle Paul. I constantly let articles on these subjects circulate among the teachers. I dare to write all this here, resting assured that nobody will mind — in order to prove that especially during that time I did not have any time to spare, nor looked for it, in order to dream in exaggerations and fantasies. And whoever looks at the works mentioned, even though fleetingly, will hardly be able to accuse me of a pathological imagination. The impressions I gained in the course of the battle were always immediate and remained not understood for a long time. I left them in their raw state for the time being, but collected them in my spirit until finally they all fit into a horrible coherence. Not until the end of the episode did I get clarity on the whole and on the details. I am now hastening toward this end, but in order to be understood, this leads me to another general survey.

For many who have heard of this case, it remains a mystery how Gottliebin, a person thinking as a Christian, and for years decided and solid, could fall into such horrible satanic temptation and in such measure. With the view in mind of solving this seeming mystery at least somewhat, I will tell what follows out of the former history of Gottliebin as I heard it from her own mouth, slowly and incoherently; I might say, by chance. Not until the end did I think that these stories were worthy of observation and full of meaning, although they lead once more into unheard of things. I trust to be forgiven the direct style, as it is more convenient.

Gottliebin knows to tell of circumstances from her childhood which point to the fact that she was lain in wait for, in order to implicate her in the net of magic. I regret to touch once more on something which as a rule is counted among the most incredible superstitions, and which I still have cause not to reject completely. Soon after her birth she was in danger of being carried away invisibly. Her mother, who died ten years ago, often told her she had the child by her side in the bed and in her sleep she suddenly feared for the child, awakened, did not feel the child and called out, "Lord Jesus, my child!" Then something fell to the floor at the bedroom door; it was the child. The same thing happened once more in a similar way. The children, who according to legend are substituted for exchange children, are destined to fall into the hands of magicians in order to be initiated early in life into the whole realm of magic. That is, if the thing has some reality, and according to conclusions to which I came through much experience. Such superstitious sounding things never had meaning for me before and did not get any meaning until in this case, when I considered the experiences with Gottliebin. Soon the child was sent to a cousin who was generally feared as an evil person, and who said once to the seven-year-old child, "When you are ten years old, I will teach you something worthwhile." This age is usually mentioned as the time of possible initiation into magic. She also said, "If you only did not have the name of Gottliebin (literally, "lover of God" or, "beloved of God") and had different godparents, I would give you great power in the world." Similar sayings caused the child concern. In her quiet thoughts she always remembered the verse, "Our Lord is great and of great power and it is beyond understanding how He rules," in the sense that really God alone is the one who rules the world. [Psalm 147:5]

The cousin died when the child was only eight years old. However, as the ignorance of the common people had made it a custom, once in a while spiritistic means and magic-like medications were used on the child when she was sick. This is why, like others, she was pulled into the net. The faculties of spirit she possessed made the instruction she received from Pastor Barth very fruitful in her heart. Her pure fear of God saved her from even deeper involvement in the sins of idolatry, and warned through pious parents, she shunned everything that tended in that direction from early in her life. However, she was already bound. I tell this according to the results which did not come out until during the course of her demonic illness. She was bound to a degree in which she was to be misused according to the principles of darkness to plague others in the spirit without having, as is always the case in a low degree of bondage, an idea or feeling of it. But her spirit, as is possible after what has been told, withstood the insinuations of darkness, through which she drew its hatred upon herself. There resulted, it appears, a sort of tension between her and the sinister realm which, as it has the desire to be unified in itself, went after her as a deserter. Now the question was to ensnare her really into magic, and at that into the deepest magic, because she only seemed safe for the devil in this way; or to do away with her lest through her resistance, a disadvantage to the sinister realm result. Therefore, Gottliebin's task — as later mine also — was faith and faithfulness, faith in the power of God to protect the believers even though all hell broke open, and faithfulness against all and every sin of idolatry. Both of these kept working together in Gottliebin and the fact that she was preserved day-by-day without having any idea of the importance, she now considers the greatest miracle done for her.

The temptations of magic came immediately upon her. Since she was very poor, her poverty was to be her destruction. By February of 1840, both her parents were already dead. She was living in the before-mentioned room, and did not have anything in the house to eat except some bread for her brother and sister, and had only ten cents. She went with that money in order to buy a pot of milk. While she was walking along, she thought, "If you only had another dime, you could get salt for the soup at the same time." She was still thinking such, when suddenly she felt two dimes in her hand. She did not feel right about it, because she remembered certain tales of magic money which are told among the common people. She was concerned about which one she was to use to pay for the milk. Fortunately the milk was given her as a gift and so she could go home with two dimes. When she crossed over a brook, her fear had risen to such a pitch that suddenly she threw the two dimes into the water and cried, "No, devil, you won't get me this way. God will see me through." She felt much lighter, but when she entered her room, the floor was covered with thaler pieces. She was frightened and moved them with her feet in order to see whether they were really thalers. She heard the ring and clearly saw their shape, and could only think that they were really money. But where did it come from? She could only be frightened at this thought, because such help did not seem divine to her. She left the room and entered again to see whether she saw right. There was nothing in the living room, but the bedroom was full of thalers. At that moment a four-year-old boy came in, and she said to him, "Go into the bedroom and what you find is yours." He came back and said, "Dear cousin, I didn't find a thing." She looked herself and indeed the thalers had vanished. Such things happened often and many times. But the slightest thought of even touching such a thaler filled her with horror, and she preferred, as she said, to remain in the most bitter poverty rather than to be made rich by the devil. Also during the time that the possessions were starting, she was tempted in this way, and before I knew of the above things, I heard the demons say, "What a shame that this girl does not want to take anything. We always put it so carefully for her." The above story of the money may have connection with this. When the floor of the bedroom was dug up, she thought she saw a capsule shimmering with thalers, and said she thought we had not looked carefully enough. Since there were rumors that the former owner of the house had once stolen 300 thalers, the possibility of finding money could not be rejected completely. Therefore, we looked once more in her presence, also with the hope of making an end of this haunting. But instead of finding money, she immediately fell into a deep unconsciousness when she pointed to the place, which indicated that the whole thing was a deception of Satan. We thought later that she was supposed to find the money secretly and keep it in order to fulfill the purpose of darkness, because secrecy and deepest concealment mark the powers of darkness in this realm. During the course of the illness, such deceptions of Satan, in order to wreck souls, were mentioned more often. The ways and means by which the real black magicians get this money or were trying to get it, according to what one demon said, are too horrible for me to tell here, although I am not afraid to tell details that may be unimportant for the understanding of my report. Most of these things I chose not to hear because I never readily believed them. Only the synthesis which developed in the course of the illness made many things meaningful which had not been so for me before. Thus it was, too, with the circumstance which follows.

After open temptations of idolatrous apostasy from God had no success with Gottliebin, the serpent showed itself even more cunning. One time Gottliebin came home when once more neither she nor her brother or sisters had any food in the house. She was disquieted and discouraged when she entered her living room. To her surprise she saw a man's shirt sleeve full of flour. Beside this, a large coin was wrapped in paper and lay on top of the flour. Made careful through former experience, she felt a horror once more. How did the flour get in? The living room was locked and it could not have been laid on the table from the window. In addition, the strange container made the gift suspicious. When she looked at the money, she read the words on the paper, "Christ's Blood and Righteousness are my adorning and dress of honor." She liked to think that way and thought, even though she did not get rid of her horrible feelings, "Well, this cannot be unrighteous, you can use this." So she kept the flour and money not without thanking God for them, although she could not discover the giver even though she asked all around. Later, however, she ascribed most of the magic spells which occurred in her to this flour, or at least, the possibility of more spells. One demon later on actually said that it all had been satanic deception, and that she should not have eaten this flour. If one wants to believe this occurrence, which is dubious in many respects, one has to assume that permission was given which had higher purposes in mind even though the use of it seemingly was highly damaging for the time being. Nevertheless, it could not be counted as actual sin, and therefore, in itself did not lead to destruction, because the sense and will remained righteous. But the test of faith now had become more difficult by a considerable degree.

These happenings give the clue, so to speak, to the whole story. To begin with, we have to do with a soul which resisted Satan although it already felt his bondage. She felt herself bound to one side, the satanic, with a certain power and her heart sought for the other side, the divine. She had to prove faithfulness and faith in order to be wrenched away from the former. Thus, the battle began, which drew ever widening circles because darkness did not want to give in, and because even in the satanic realm one member hangs together with the others, and everything is very closely related. Thus, no matter how insignificant the individual was, all of hell could be stirred up by and by. The battle even became the cause by which the satanic realm received not a small blow concerning its mysterious powers. After Gottliebin had proved faith and faithfulness in the first beginnings, these demands eventually came upon me. They consisted in not allowing the attacked person to become the victim of darkness at any price. I could only do this by not trying any other means except prayer, which held fast to the invisible divine power. Satan was constantly trying to do away with Gottliebin's life, especially when the secret of the satanic deception became more and more evident. This seemed especially to infuriate the demons. Also, there was the fact that the satanic power of magic was in danger of being destroyed forever, because it was overcome in the right way. According to perceptions which I did not make until later, and especially towards the end, involuntarily and nearly forcibly this became clear. For this reason, a removal of the person seemed to become ever more necessary in order that the dark powers could make their survival sure. As for the latter, it was only too obvious that every hidden power of magic exhausted itself in this person. In order to help her as much as possible, which would not have been possible if she had died - I ask to be pardoned the expression – ever new batteries were moved into the battle for her life. Since my courage and strength grew, the demons were vanquished. I consider this the greatest miracle, because I can only think that it was a special grace of God given to me for this battle. One bulwark of magic after another had to sink into the dust, until finally the main blow was dealt at the end, when the head of all satanic magic powers seemed to come on the scene. I write unheard of thoughts here, but He who was my shield and protection and who knows my heart, knows how slowly and with what distaste I came to them, and how difficult it is for me to write the whole account down exactly because of the apparent meaning of the battle. But I cannot possibly keep it quiet unless the whole is to appear as a nearly senseless mystery.

The attacks on Gottliebin's life became more gruesome every day. As every object smuggled into her body had the purpose of killing her, she also tried much to commit suicide, as a rule, however, without being conscious of it. Besides what was told above, she hanged herself once in the woods with her scarf. Without knowing what she was doing, she carried together stones in order to hang high enough and then she tied the scarf artfully to the tree. She had already hung herself, when the scarf broke and the violent fall brought her to. On the same evening, without my knowing the above, one demon called out of her, "What a shame that this girl cannot be killed. She hanged herself and the rope had to break." More than once she had violent hemorrhages, during which she not only came close to death, but seemed to have fallen prey to death already. Also, when she vomited, many times breath and pulse would disappear for several minutes, and her face showed the signs of death. Once, and I had rather tell the whole story, although this will be the hardest part to believe, she wanted to make a hole into her womb in order to make way for a needle that was in her.

She was only half conscious. She cut the knife into her womb and it was a pleasure for her to burrow her insides with the knife until the stomach was pierced. Thereupon all the food she had eaten came out of the stomach area. Her friends testified to that and the doctor saw the wound at such a time as to be convinced by its aspect of the truth of what was told. For the time being the wound could not be fatal because it was not her deed; therefore, divine deliverance intervened. But it could become and had to become fatal if faith had not taken hold of the almighty power of God. Once all her wounds, also the last mentioned, suddenly broke open again and the danger had risen to the extreme. I remained in the faith, which never let me down. When a friend rushed to me in greatest consternation and reported that each minute of delay was dangerous, I fell on my knees in my room, completely affected, and spoke bold words. So strong did I become at this moment that this time I did not even want to do the devil the honor of going there. I told the friend to tell Gottliebin to get up and come to me. She could do so by faith. It was not long before she came up the stairs of my house, but nobody will ever know how I felt. By the way, here, as on other occasions, several days were needed for the complete healing. Beside the many other things I could mention, I will mention only what a demon said, which identified itself as a medical doctor who had died forty years ago in Hamburg. It also mentioned its name and said it had slowly charmed no less than six measures of poison into her. This could explain why all the blood and all the liquid she vomited had a pungent and highly repugnant smell, which I did not know to compare with anything similar, and which I encountered only once later on in a possessed boy who thought he was poisoned. In all of these and similar things the name of Jesus overcame, sometimes only the mention of the promise in Mark 16 or the verse in Philippians 2.

The desired end of the story came during last Christmas (24th to 28th of December of 1843) when everything that had happened before seemed to come together once more. The worst part was that in those days the sinister influence also worked on the half-blind brother and another sister, Katharina, so that I had to fight the most desperate battle with three at the same time. The inner connection was clearly seen. I cannot tell how the course of details went. It was too manifold for me to keep everything in my memory. But they were days the like of which I hope never to live through again. It had come to the point that I had to risk everything as if to say, to overcome or to die. As great as my effort was, I clearly felt a divine protection so that I did not feel the slightest tiredness or weariness, not even after forty hours of waking, fasting, and wrestling. The brother was free the fastest, and in such a way that he could immediately help me actively from then on. The worst attack did not come on Gottliebin this time. She seemed to be completely free during the last act, after battles had been fought before. The worst attack came on her sister Katharina, who had never before experienced the least of such things. But now she raged in such a way that she could only be held with difficulty. She threatened to tear me into a thousand pieces, and I could not dare to step too close to her. She made incessant attempts to tear up her womb with her own hands, as she said, or looked around cunningly as if she wanted to do something horrible to those who held her. She chattered and cried so terribly during that time that one could think of thousands of blasphemous mouths united in hers. The most striking thing was that she remained completely conscious, so that one could talk to her, and so that she said, when strongly admonished, that she could not act or talk in any other way, and to please hold her quite firmly lest anything happen through her. And even afterwards she had the clearest memory of everything, even of the most horrible attempts of murder. These memories affected her so depressingly that I had to take special care of her for several days, until after much and serious prayer her memories slowly faded. At the same time, however, the demon spoke out of her equally firmly. It did not identify itself as the spirit of a deceased human being this time, but as a prominent angel of Satan, as the chiefest of all magic, which had received power from Satan for this work and through whom this hellish work had found ramifications in various directions for the furtherance of the satanic reign. It stated that the deadly blow to magic was given now that it had to go into the abyss, and that magic would slowly bleed to death because of this blow. Suddenly, toward twelve o'clock midnight, it seemed as though it beheld the open fiery abyss. Then out of the girl's throat roared several times and lasting about a quarter of an hour, only one cry of despair with such violent strength that it seemed the house would collapse. Nothing more horrible can be thought of, and it could not be but that half of the town's inhabitants got knowledge of the battle, not without special fright. Katharina was seized with such violent shakings that it was as if she would shake off every limb individually. Even though the demon seemed to be all fear and despair, its defiance was nonetheless no less gigantic, and it demanded of God to be given a sign, because it would not go out until a sign had been given from heaven that would shake the entire town so that it would not have to lay down its role as commonly as other sinners, but so to speak, go to hell with honors. Such a horrifying mixture of despair, malice, defiance, and pride has hardly ever been seen anywhere. In the meantime, its expected destruction seemed to be prepared ever more rapidly in the unseen world. Finally, the most moving moment came, which no one can possibly imagine adequately who was not an eye and ear witness. At two o'clock in the morning the supposed angel of Satan roared, while the girl bent her head and upper part of her body back over the backrest of the chair, with a voice of which one could hardly have believed a human throat capable, "Jesus is Victor! Jesus is Victor!" – words that sounded so far and were understood at such a distance that they made an unforgettable impression on many people. Now the power and strength of the demon seemed to be broken more with every moment. It became ever more quiet and calmer, could only make a few motions and finally disappeared unnoticed like the life-light of a dying person goes out; however, not until eight o'clock in the morning.

That was the point at which the battle of two years came to an end. I was so sure and certain that this was so that I could not but let my triumphant joy be noticed the following day, Sunday, when I had to preach on the Magnificat of Mary. Of course, there were a number of things which had to be cleared up afterwards, but it was only the debris of a building that had collapsed. I hardly had any more work with the half-blind brother, a modest and humble man of much Christian understanding who had much faith and power of prayer. The satanic attack which came upon him had hardly been noticed by other people. Katharina had spasms once in a while for some time due to the extraordinary effect upon her soul, but soon was completely restored. I would say that no one has heard what happened to her. Gottliebin was somewhat more affected in the time following, but they were only renewed attempts of darkness, failing by themselves, with former things, which did not take up much of my time. While these stray attacks occurred, it happened that she slowly came to complete health. All her former illnesses, which are well known to the doctors, were completely healed: the high side, the short foot, the stomach trouble, etc. Meanwhile, her health became ever stronger and more durable. And for some time now it has been so with her, that completely restored, she can be considered a real miracle of God. Her Christian disposition has increased to a pleasant degree, and she has become a blessed tool in many hearts through her quiet humility, her solid and understanding way of talking, her decisiveness and her modesty. The thing that shows best the worth of her character is that I do not know of any other female person who would know how to deal with children with as much insight, love, patience and kindness as Gottliebin. For this reason, I prefer to leave my children with her above anyone else, when help is needed. During the past year she was a teacher of industry to the fullest satisfaction. I can only think with most grateful surprise of the preserving divine providence, because of which it was not necessary even one single time to cancel classes, though the time was very hard otherwise. Now that a school for small children is to be built, I cannot find a person who would be as suitable as she to lead this school.

Möttlingen, the 11th of August 1844.
Pastor Johann Christoph Blumhardt

POSTSCRIPT

As six full years have passed since the above report was written, the reader will be anxious to hear how Gottliebin is now. I simply state that she moved into my house for good, four years ago. She is the most faithful and most understanding help to my wife in housekeeping and child education. My wife can entrust her by all means with everything in the housekeeping department, small and big things, and can leave her in charge of it if circumstances so require. I will let others testify as to what she is to us and to all those who come into our house, because I know that no one who comes to know her will fail to speak everywhere of his respect and esteem for her. She has just about become indispensable to me in the treatment of mentally ill people, since they soon find unlimited confidence in her so that my work with them requires only little time. By the way, she is not with us as a servant, because her gratitude will not allow her to be paid for that which she does for us. Rather she considers herself adopted as a child, which is now also the case with her sister Katharina and her half-blind brother.

Möttlingen, the 31st of July, 1850.
Pastor Johann Christoph Blumhardt

ABOUT THE AUTHOR

Johann Christoph Blumhardt was born on the 16th of July, 1805, to poor and pious artisans in Stuttgart, Germany. His gifts were developed extraordinarily early in life. He went to school at the age of three; later to college and university. After having passed his theological exams well, he became vicar in the town of Dürrenmenz in Württemberg, then teacher in the mission house in Basle, then assistant pastor in Iptingen. On the 31st of July, 1838, he became pastor in Möttlingen near Calw, at that time a village of 535 souls. Here he had the three great experiences of his life that have become of special importance, not only for his entire life's work, which was to follow, but also — as he was convinced — for the kingdom of God. The first one he called, "The Battle." The second experience was a movement of repentance and awakening, and the third, connected with the first two, the continual miracle of an answered prayer and healing for the sick. For him this was nothing else than the "experience of the real presence of the Lord Jesus." Thus miracles became natural for him.

Out of these experiences proceeded the extraordinary forming and molding of his personality that made him the eminent minister, preacher and author which he was. Exactly fourteen years later, on the 31st of July, 1852, he moved with his family to Bad Boll at the foot of the Swabian Alb. He was able to acquire a property for 25,000 florins, although he himself only had 400 florins, in order to continue his ministry there, especially for the sick for whom there was no hope left. People of every social standing streamed to him, as they did before in Möttlingen for nearly ten years, from all sides and often from the farthest distances, who sought consolation, alleviation and help through his encouragement, preaching and prayerful compassion. Blumhardt was filled with the hope of the kingdom of God coming soon and of the glorious victory of God's mercy over all nations, as few others were. On the 25th of February, 1880, he went into the joy of his Lord after he blessed his son Christoph Friedrich Blumhardt with his last strength as his successor and victor.

JESUS CASTS OUT DEMONS

(Matthew 8:29-32)

Jesus treibet Teufel aus.

Und siehe, sie schrieen und sprachen: ach Jesu, du Sohn GOTTES, was haben wir mit dir zu thun? Bist du herkommen, uns zu quälen, ehe denn es Zeit ist? Es war aber ferne von ihnen eine große Heerde Säue an der Weide. Da baten ihn die Teufel und sprachen: willt du uns austreiben, so erlaube uns in die Heerde Säue zu fahren. Und er sprach: fahret hin.

Ev. Matthäi. Cap. 8. v. 29—32.

Die Bibel in Bildern
Julius Schnorr von Carolsfeld
(1794 - 1872)

www.ingramcontent.com/pod-product-compliance
Lightning Source LLC
La Vergne TN
LVHW041456190726
843491LV00008B/2396